everything is a big deal

for an ocean

susan bruce

Finishing Line Press

Georgetown, Kentucky

everything is a big deal

for an ocean

Publisher: Leah Huete de Maines

Editor: Christen Kincaid

Book Design and Cover Photo: Pascale Willi

Author Photo: Amanda Moffatt

Order online: www.finishinglinepress.com

also available on amazon.com

Author inquiries and mail orders:

Finishing Line Press

P. O. Box 1626

Georgetown, Kentucky 40324

U.S.A.

To Peter, Simon and Lucas

Table of Contents

Part I

Part II

If a story is not about the hearer he will not listen.

—John Steinbeck, East of Eden

Part I

Ocean addresses the writer
because she sits on the beach and stares at the water.

An Agreement

We've had lot of playtime you and I
a lot of sleepovers, am I right?
You are the drawing of a woman
pulled in endless directions.
I'm blue under blue
a voice from out of the ground
jumping off every impulse
unfolding in opposites.
I come apart. I leave. I reenter.
It would seem like
we could be blissful together.

Four Billion Years Ago

Why I was once a boiling pond laced with cyanide condensed
into a red hot pool of rain perched on the horizon that today
I call self.

Why I am blue waiting for a feeling that I am not a mistake.
Why I am a monster in a soft blue leotard.

Wave 1

The storm is a tough neighborhood
absent light with its eyes poked out.

The sounds become a noisy aphrodisiac
as in *hahahahahahahahahahahahahahaha*.

I last remember dirty business, staring at nipples, reversing them,
chucking a chair out the window then rocking a baby.

The sun has been obscured by fathomless fog.
I want a flashbulb of joy to charge at me. I need the sun.

Wave 2

I live like a soft plaything in rain.
My heart has a banshee mouth and patriarch eyes.
I have never gently held a plum.

Wave 3

As a wave artist I sprinkle cells of splash.
I'm left to sing when the sun rises
and sing when the sun sets.

Am I to take pleasure singing when
my ancient instinct clenches air and coerces ice?
Who bends the light so that I'm seen, so that I'm heard?

Wave 4

I imagine when my head falls the dead talk.
I am always hungry. I take possession
of what there is to put in my mouth *yes*,
in fear of deflating, *yes*, to separate Friday
from Saturday *yes*, before the pearly gates close
and *yes*, I give it all to myself.
I am an orphan and a drop out. I pledge
to growl and burst, *knock down then enter*
taught to me by a long line of waves.
The moment I stop sounding like the planets
are oscillating, something is wrong.

Wave 5

I convince myself
I'm not alone, not lost,
by bumping into stuff
a dozen shipwrecks
50,000 autos, 50,000 straws
50,000 balloons, 50,000 footballs
and half-buried glass bottles
that croak like grackles.
This cluttered ribcage.

Ocean Confessions

I can lie around in a coma on an old mattress
surrounded by used tissues capable of eternity.

I cannot express what I mean.
I'm not sure what I mean. No one tells me anything.

I repeat I repeat like a playground swing.
The do-overs become drifts. The drops keep dripping.

I have so many giant boobs I can hardly watch the ground.
Everybody knows how half-light that is.

How unwieldy these wings, this wild knowing.
I will run a bath now.

Certain Facts a Wave Cannot Control

I am the middle of the eye.

Pouring water on my face.

Looking like a 1940's movie star.

I am a star fruit trying to be edible.

I go blind.

I'm busy blowing off time.

Walking underwater.

Nodding at every wave.

No brakes.

Folk Song

The blue the blue the midnight blue
the grey indigo cobalt
the teal the turquoise the navy the black
the silvery grey the bluet
the navy the grey indigo blue
the bright the light the black
the marine azure the teal blue grey
the midnight dark water bluet

Ice Cubes

It was I, not the sky, who lifted the rocks
and carried them like they were thin wafers.
And it is I who will move them again
just to watch the ocean lose track of itself.
I did that. I take what has always been mine.
I will go to hell for dismantling the universe.

Wave 6

Consider Baptism.

The moment Jesus came out of the water
he saw the sky split open and God's spirit
looked like a dove along with a voice saying
*you are my son, chosen and marked by my love
pride of my life.*
However, it was the water that said
*Come with me
whoever is baptized is saved.*

Wave 7

I realize my chromosomal experience of wavy
is a secret you either get or don't get, the way
stars are fed by cabbage butterflies at night.
Wavy is crossing one wave over another
like legs interwoven.
I say good morning to every pelting wave.
Do you expect me to act as if we live together?

Wave 8

Each day is a notable 100-foot wave
that will be left behind. The ocean is
only a body of days staring at the sky
overflowing into a teapot.

Wave 9

My unfastened thoughts
(think wave thinking wave)
park and stay
like carved pieces of hell
I can't stop telling myself.
I hold my head in my hands
and stare at the cacophony
like it's a creature
pulling down my socks.
I let off steam
and ejaculate more waves.

I Call the Secret

I am life and death without a single scratch

an engine that doesn't hurt day.

When I dream of you, you unbutton your shirt.

Pat me anywhere as much as you like.

Talking is too grown up for me.

I will be foul and remember this feeling.

I will try not to hold you down.

Part II

The writer considers that everything is a big deal for the ocean.

Hoping to Be Rescued

Dear Ocean, this is how it happens.
You bloom. We roll
indistinguishable from sleep.
I'm stripped of my hoodie.
You get lucky.
You hug my legs.
Your arms fuss with my arms,
                    fluster my hair.
I forget I ever trusted anything.
I turn into the shape of shivering
and remember when we met
the feel of sea power born on my skin.
                    I was ten years old
wearing a bikini that wouldn't stay on.
You are a gangster
running a racket of disorderly waves.
You are neither painting, nor poem
                    of an ocean.
Your trapdoor, always open.

Splash Notes

One wave throbs and spits in my eye.

One wave gives up and hands itself over to wet Jesus.

One wave comes undone, falls to its knees shrieking.

One wave has a sinking feeling and goes to pieces like war.

One wave is pecked by ghosts of rain but looks like a hill of ruffles.

One wave believes in nothing but magic.

One wave is the likeness of a rocket ship looking down.

One wave likes ice cubes.

One wave hates to be touched.

Many waves are siblings every morning.

One wave smiles like a valuable.

One wave dreams of getting out of her portable basket.

One wave taps maple syrup from the stern of an oil tanker.

One wave is the great-great-grand wave of Hurricane Sandy.

One wave blusters like a volcano. That's the wave to fear.

One wave considers itself immortal.

Waves are born to break open and find each other, like victory songs.

Clearing Up the Question of the Ocean's Blindness

If the ocean is blind, then it squints into space
assessing that each star could've been a wave.

If the ocean has always been blind, then it acts
to counteract the fatigue of agonizingly slow forays
from New York to the United Kingdom and back.

If the ocean cannot turn off its water, then it expresses
flickering feelings such as I'm-out-of-control or
what's-wrong-with-you or catch-me-if-you-can.

If the ocean is blind to itself, then it has an undeveloped ego
that creates a condition of nonstop feats of gymnastics and
blindness is its perception.

If perception is to have fun, then blindness is foolish and
the ocean is a predator tromping around amassing species,
not letting them go home.

If the rotund ocean expands and engulfs blindly and its
central nervous system is disrupted, then the ocean will
trick, cheat, and deceive.

The Writer Addresses Wave and Wave Responds

Sometimes the idea of the ocean scares me shitless.

Think of me as a friendly mall wave.

How do you feel about darkness?

The unseeable feels pointless, even fatal.

Have you ever stayed more than one night in one place?

It's not possible. I wander and re-establish.

Can you exist untroubled for one night?

Yes. I enjoy an intoxicating storm surge
and aspire to be a skyscraper.

What do you want people to say about you?

It's nice you are still here.

What does the passage of time mean to you?

My body passing through breakage autonomy.
My body a minivan in a riot.

Can I trust you will be kind to me?

I can only be careful how I fool around
when I'm not in a strange wind.

Wave Notebook

Waves want to happen. They gesture to imaginary places.
I sit on the sidelines and watch persona connecting the dots.

~

Waves want an identity. Each has been spilled from
a different package of truth: roaring-ambulance wave,
prized-for-its-support-of the-whale wave, chew-the-nuts-
spit-out-the-boat wave, full-speed-ahead wave, bedspread
wave, where-has-Amelia-Earhart-gone wave...

~

We humans, who are perceived in understanding
                    fall head to head and temper to temper
                              like splash falls onto itself.

~

If the sea is too tightly packed, too many blockbusters
the ocean becomes bedlam, and yet I still say
all waves live well together.

Here

I sit by an ocean
as it opens and closes
all its doors, in a dress
I was poured into
hundreds of years ago
before I ever knew
I might feel cold water
touch my face
this close
then this close.
Water is death abiding
or singing on my mouth.

Yes, And

Let me move my mind
into 50 degree water
yes, and
so that I can feel my bones
my cheeks stinging
in quill cold
my clean face untended.
I say to my thin skin
have compassion for the coldness
as if it is human
or a close-eyed earwig
or the cool of a full throated choir
cleaved to my body.
Why do I endure such cold?
So that I can grow and be changed
so that I can hear myself say
to the comedian of icy coldness
to that lazy order of things
yes, and.

After Forty Years of Swimming and Ten Years Surfing

I enter the water.
It passes close enough
to kiss me.
It feels like old love.
Stay I say to the very small wave
so dense in salt I can float on my back
on its back.
We are traveling as one, one passport.
Once I thought the ocean was god
and I was just a frightened little girl.
A wave is just a flower
with many little flowers hidden inside it.
I stand on top of a wave as it shatters.
I slide down its serpentine back.
I'm swimming in a spiderweb of blue joy
in my most present nowness.

Acknowledgments

My deepest appreciation to Matthew Lippman, for escorting these wave poems from Covid into broad day light, for always encouraging me to keep land in sight. This book would not exist without your support.

Thank you to my writers group, for tirelessly listening to more water poems than anyone can imagine; Leah Umansky, Wendy Weinstein, Bergen Huttaff, Sarah Paley, Beth Dufford and Heather Newman.

Thank you Pascale Willi for giving this book beauty.

Thank you Holly Scott. Nothing happens in this storm without you and your joy.

Thank you, Alice Kaltman. You are the beginning and epicenter of my ocean devotion.

And finally, unending love and gratitude to my husband Peter for believing in me through plays and poems. Thank you, Simon and Lucas, for always showing up with humor, honesty, and for everything else. My love for you has no bounds.

About the Author

For over twenty years Susan Bruce was an actress in NYC. She acted on and off Broadway, in the original production of *Angels in America* and in *The Women* during the months following 9/11, which is when she began writing. Susan studied poetry at The New School with Patricia Carlin and Kathleen Ossip. Her poetry has appeared in Love's *Executive Order, Washington Square Review, Arcturus, Driftwood Press, december, Channel Magazine, Barrow Street*.

In her first chapbook, *Body of Water*, Bruce explored a fear of deep water which she later challenged by leaning to surf. In this book Bruce invents a conversation between wave and writer, as a discourse on everything human.

Bruce received an MFA from Tisch School of the Arts and a BA from University of Michigan. She is married to the film maker Peter Hedges. They split their time between Brooklyn and Montauk, and have two sons, Simon and Lucas.

www.ingramcontent.com/pod-product-compliance
Lightning Source LLC
Chambersburg PA
CBHW022055080426
42734CB00009B/1363